THE CLASSIC ART OF
HAND
SHADOWS

ANIMALS • BIRDS • FACES

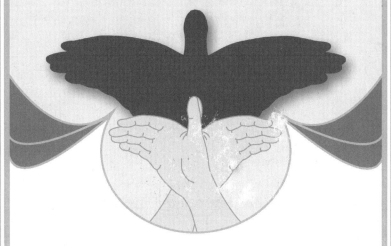

A collection of classic shadow figures
that you form with your hands.

WITH ILLUSTRATED INSTRUCTIONS

Algrove Publishing

Algrove Publishing Limited
36 Mill Street, P.O. Box 1238
Almonte, Ontario, Canada K0A 1A0

Telephone: (613) 256-0350
Fax: (613) 256-0360
Email: sales@algrove.com
Web: www.algrove.com

Library and Archives Canada Cataloguing in Publication

The classic art of hand shadows.

Includes index.
ISBN 978-1-897030-63-9

1. Shadow-pictures. I. Title.

GV1218.S5C54 2007   791.5'3   C2007-904341-0

Printed in Canada
#2-10-07

Table of Contents

Continued on next page

Introduction

Historians believe that hand shadows or "shadowgraphs" have been around since about 850 AD. Although the popularity of this art form has come and gone over the centuries, many people continued trying new ways of positioning their hands in an effort to create novel images. The result is a long list of classic hand shadows. This book will introduce you to some of the classic images as well as a few newer ones. We have added suggestions on ways of making some of the figures appear life-like but with some experimentation you may find other ways to do this and create your own hand shadows.

Since hands and fingers come in a range of different sizes, shapes and levels of flexibility, you may find that some shadow figures will be easy to form, while others will prove to be more difficult—some may seem downright impossible! Don't be discouraged. With a bit of patience and practice, positioning your hands and fingers becomes easier and you will soon learn to master most of the shadows.

The great advantage of this art form is the fact that little is needed except a light source, a flat, light-coloured surface for the screen, some imagination, and your hands!

Tools You Will Need

A Light Source

Choose a light source bright enough to cast a sharp shadow. The brighter the light, the sharper the shadow. One method would be to lay a bright flashlight (aimed at the screen) on a table or have someone with a steady hand hold it for you (This is a good method if you are camping. You can use the tent wall as a screen.).

One of the best light sources is a goose-neck desk lamp. The flexible arm makes it easy to direct the light at a screen and its shade will keep the bright light out of your audience's eyes.

A Screen

A smooth, light coloured wall makes a suitable screen on which to cast shadows or you can simply attach a large sheet of smooth white paper to the wall. Even a crease-free white pillowcase or tablecloth will do.
TIP: The reverse side of a roll of gift wrapping paper is usually smooth and white. Cut off the size you need for your screen and hang it on the wall.

Your Hands

We recommend that you start with clean, dry hands. If not, you may find it hard to hold some of the positions if your fingers or hands are sticking or slipping (keep a soft cloth nearby to wipe your hands if they become damp and sticky during your show). The key to making a good hand shadow is having flexible fingers. Practice will help you to achieve this.

CAUTION

When using a lamp light source, make sure it has a non-tip base and that it is set up on a flat sturdy surface. Avoid fire hazards by setting up the light source well away from any flammable objects or surfaces. Keep your hands and clothing off the hot surface of the light bulb to avoid burns. Turn the light source off when you leave your stage setup unattended.
DO NOT USE CANDLES OR ANY LIVE FLAME AS A LIGHT SOURCE.

What You Should Know About Making Hand Shadows

A shadow is cast when the path of light rays is blocked. The strength, distance, and size of the light source will change how the shadow looks.

Experiment on where best to position your light source and hands. For instance, you can start with your light source three feet away from the screen. Position your hands in the center of that three-foot distance. Now move your hands slowly toward the screen to see what happens to the shadow and then move your hands slowly back toward your light source. The shadow you cast will become smaller, darker and crisper as you move towards the screen and it will become larger and softer looking as you move towards your light source. You can also experiment on moving your light source forward and back from the screen to see how this will affect the shadows you cast. This book can not give you specific measurements, as each light source will have a different degree of brightness or size and some rooms may be darker than others. These factors will alter the way your shadows will look.

When you cast a shadow that you are happy with, make note of your distances for the next time. When you set up in a different place, you can use these measurements as a starting point and make adjustments from there.

View of a basic stage setup from above.

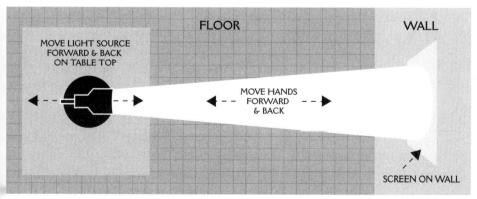

MOVE LIGHT SOURCE FORWARD & BACK ON TABLE TOP

FLOOR

WALL

MOVE HANDS FORWARD & BACK

SCREEN ON WALL

Setting Up a Stage

Choose a room for your stage set up that can be darkened. The darker the room, the better your hand shadows will look.

Some hand shadow positions will have you working toward one edge of the screen or the other. If you position yourself to the right of the wall screen, sit the audience more to the left. If you work on the left side of the wall screen, let the audience sit on the right. When you use the Backlit Stage setup (#3), the audience can sit directly in front of you.

The following are ways to set up a staging area. Take the time to experiment with the positions of the light source and your hands, to see what distances are best.

1. Basic Hand Shadow Stage

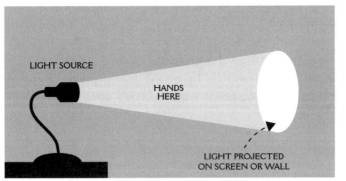

LIGHT SOURCE

HANDS
HERE

LIGHT PROJECTED
ON SCREEN OR WALL

HOW IT LOOKS

This is the basic hand shadow stage that is easy to set up just about anywhere. All you need is a light source, a screen, and your hands.

2. Framed Hand Shadow Stage

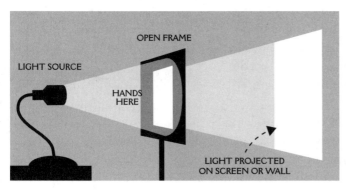

A clever way to focus attention on the hand shadow figures is to use a shadow frame. You can cut one out of a stiff piece of cardboard. The inside of the frame can be cut to a round or square shape. The size of the frame should leave enough room for hand shadow movements. It can be suspended from the ceiling, held by a tripod, attached to the edge of a table, or you can build a stand for it.

ROUND SHADOW
FRAME

Aim your light source at the open area inside the frame and line up your screen with that light. Your hands should be close to the frame to get the full effect.

3. Backlit Hand Shadow Stage

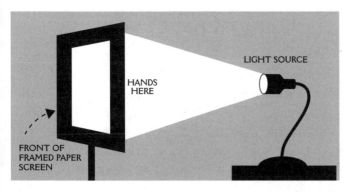

The backlit stage is a bit more work but it is the best stage setup for the hand shadow artist and the audience. The difference is that you are not casting the hand shadow onto a wall screen; you are casting it onto a small free-standing backlit screen that faces the audience.

Continued on next page

Making the Backlit Frame

Cut a frame out of a stiff piece of card-board. The inside of the frame can be cut to a round or square shape. The size of the frame should leave enough room for hand shadow movements inside it.

Once your frame is cut out, you will need a piece of regular white bond paper (the same as typing paper) or a heavier tissue paper that will fit the frame size. You should not be able to see through the paper but the light should show through. Fit this paper to the card-board frame. Tape or glue the paper to it.

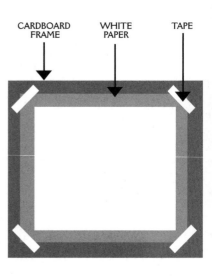

CARDBOARD FRAME   WHITE PAPER   TAPE

It is best positioned on a tripod that can be easily adjusted. Another option would be to build a base for the frame and set it on a stand or table.

Aim a bright light source at the paper area inside the frame. Your hands need to be VERY close to the paper to get the full affect of the hand shadow. One of the good things about this stage method is that whatever shadow you see cast at the back of the frame is the shadow that your audience will see at the front of the frame....in reverse!

Using Props

When working on a show, it helps to use props with your hand shadows. For example, you could have an assistant hold a cardboard dog bone and you could show a German Shepherd taking it into his mouth. Another idea would be to have an assistant hold a carrot under the rabbit's nose and you could make it appear to be munching on it. The goose could be made to look as though it has a great big worm in its beak by using a thick piece of knitting wool or string as a prop. Use your voice to mimic the sounds of the figures or have music playing while you are performing your show. The use of props and sound can make your hand shadow show unique and entertaining.

ALLIGATOR

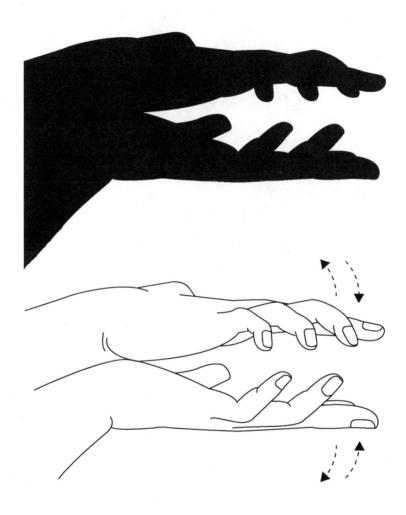

SUGGESTIONS: You can make the alligator appear to be snapping its jaws by rolling your hands open and closed while your wrists stay touching (keep your fingers in the same position). You can also slowly move the shadow figure forward on the screen making it appear to be an alligator on the hunt.

BEAR CUB

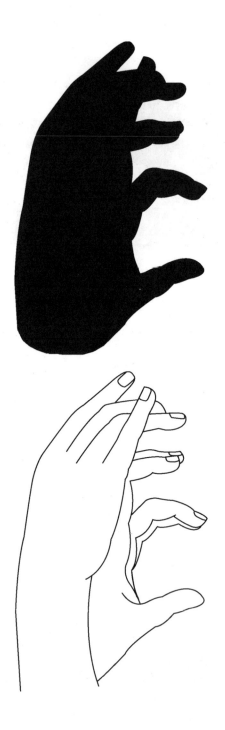

BILLY GOAT

SUGGESTIONS: With a little practice, you can mimic a billy goat. To make his ear twitch, just move the thumb of your right hand up and down. To make his beard sway in the wind, make slight movements with the little finger of your left hand. You will notice that when you move your little finger, your ring finger will move slightly, making the goat look like he is chewing.

BULL DOG

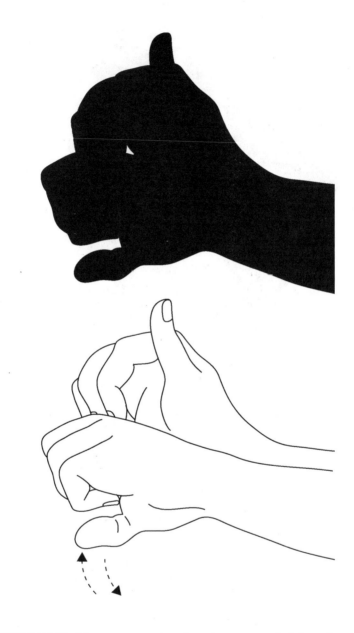

SUGGESTIONS: If you move the thumb on your left hand up and down you can make the dog appear to be eating or barking. If you make a barking sound at the same time as the mouth appears to be moving, it will make the hand shadow more realistic.

CAMEL

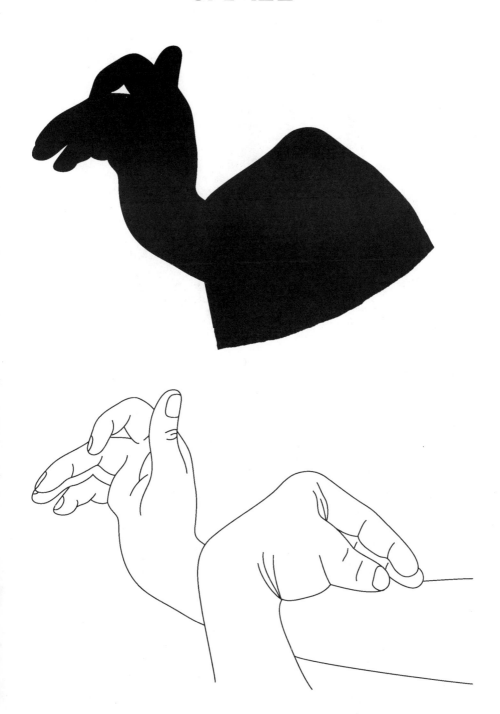

COW

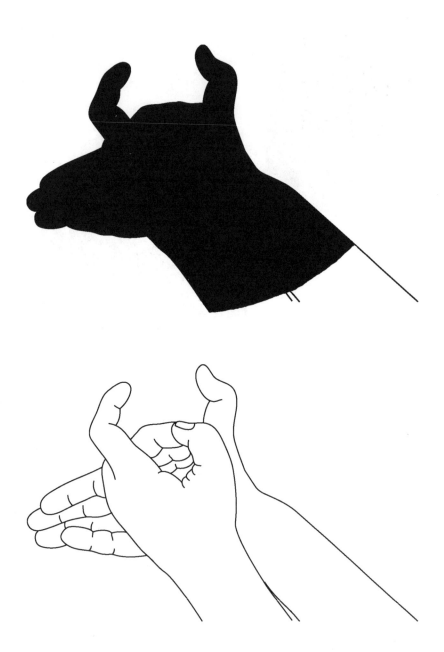

CRAB

SUGGESTIONS: To make the crab appear life-like, simply move all of your fingers (not your thumbs) as if it is crawling along the screen. Crabs sometimes move sideways too. This will make your shadow figure look more realistic.

DEER

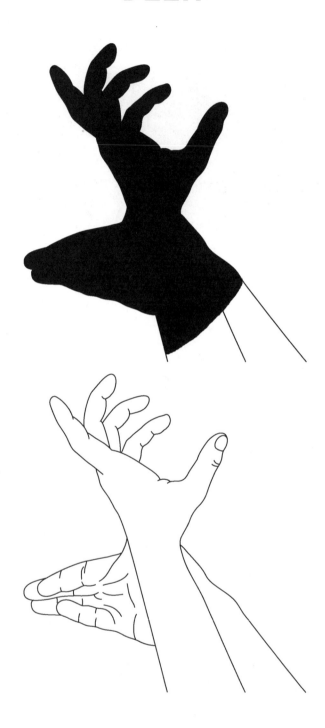

DINOSAUR

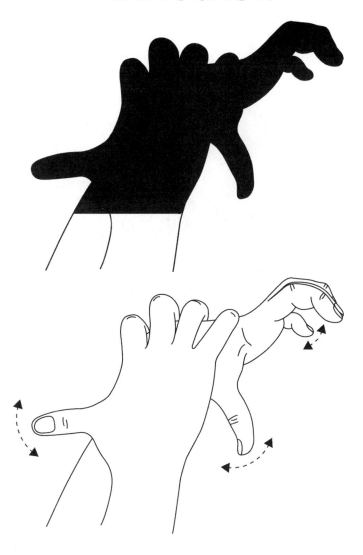

SUGGESTIONS: To make the dinosaur move its arms and tail, move your thumbs up and down. With practice, you can make it appear to be roaring by moving the little finger of the left hand up and down. Give it some life by moving the creature forward with slow up and down movements as if it were lumbering on the forest floor. At the same time, tap your foot loudly on the floor as you make a down movement to mimic the heavy sound the creature would make when walking. Stop every now and then to move the arms and tail and let out a roar.

DOG

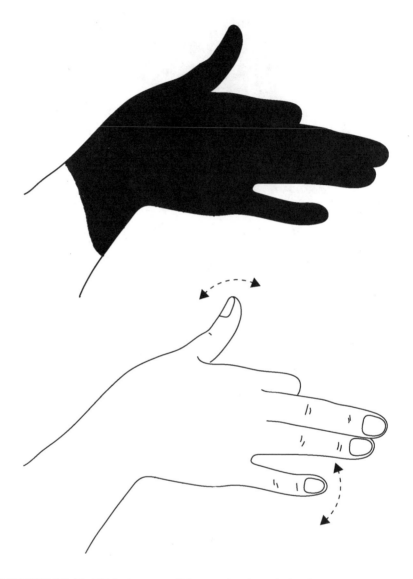

SUGGESTIONS: This is one of the easier hand shadows to master since it requires only one hand. Move your thumb to twitch the ears around. With a bit of concentration and practice, you can move your little finger up and down to make the dog's mouth move. If you can hold your position, you can make this dog look up and down and bark at the same time.

DOG BEGGING

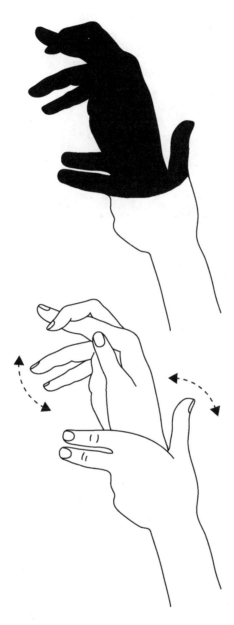

SUGGESTIONS: You can make this dog beg by moving the ring and little fingers of your right hand up and down at the same time. Wag the dog's tail by moving the thumb of your left hand up and down. Make this character more realistic by making whining sounds as a dog would.

DONKEY

SUGGESTIONS: If done well, this hand shadow becomes everyone's funny favourite. Twitch the donkey's ears by moving the first and middle fingers of the right hand. To make the mouth open and close you will have to open the middle and ring fingers of the left hand WHILE holding the overlapped fingers in position (see diagram in circle). Practice this so that you can sound out a loud "hee haw...hee haw" while opening and closing the mouth and twitching the ears all around.

ELEPHANT

SUGGESTIONS: You can control the elephant's trunk by swinging the middle and ring fingers of the left hand forward and back. To show a chewing movement, simply swing the thumb of the left hand. To show the appearance of walking, move the shadow in a forward motion across the screen adding the slight up and down movements of this large animal.

GERMAN SHEPHERD DOG

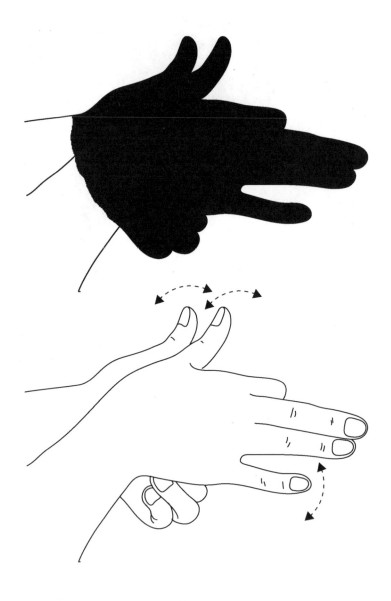

SUGGESTIONS: If you can fake a good bark, making this hand shadow come to life will be no problem. With a bit of practice you can move the little finger of your right hand up and down to open and close the mouth. Wiggling the thumbs of both hands will move the dog's ears.

GOAT KID

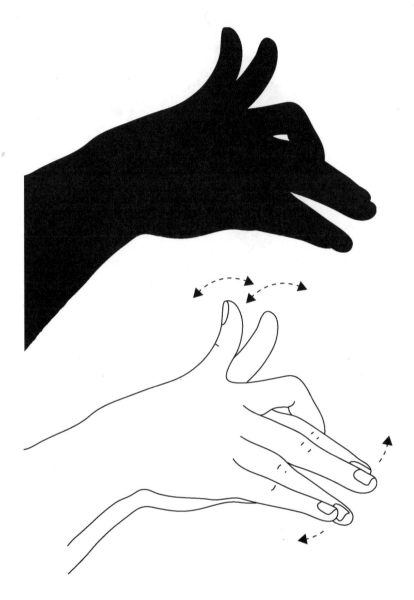

SUGGESTIONS: If you have ever seen a curious goat kid, you know that they move around a lot. Mastering several movements at once can be difficult at first but with a bit of practice you may be able to move the head, ears, and mouth at the same time. If you can also make a bleating sound, this hand shadow will take on a life of its own.

GREYHOUND

SUGGESTIONS: Just like the German Shepherd on page 20, making this hand shadow come to life will be no problem. With a bit of practice you can move the little finger of your left hand up and down to open and close the mouth. Wiggle your thumb to move the dog's ear.

HORSE

SUGGESTIONS: This beautiful hand shadow is easy to make. To twitch the horse's ears, simply move both the thumbs. To open and close the mouth, open the middle and ring fingers of the left hand WHILE holding the overlapped fingers in position (see diagram in circle). Practice this so that you can roll the head back and whinny, neigh, and blow like a horse. Roll the nose downward (while holding the position) and make the horse appear to be eating grass.

KANGAROO

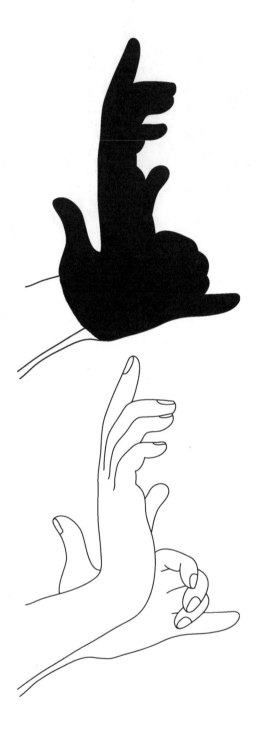

MOOSE

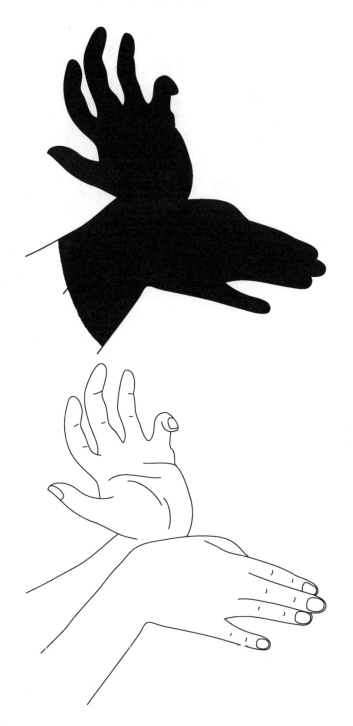

PANTHER

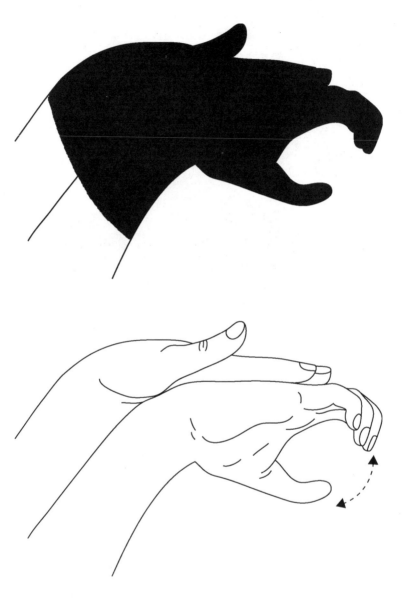

SUGGESTIONS: Making this panther take a big bite is easy. While holding the position of your two hands firm, you can open and close the fingers to the thumb of your right hand. To mimic the movement of this big cat, start with a slow forward motion across the screen and then a quick pounce while closing the jaw.

PIGLET

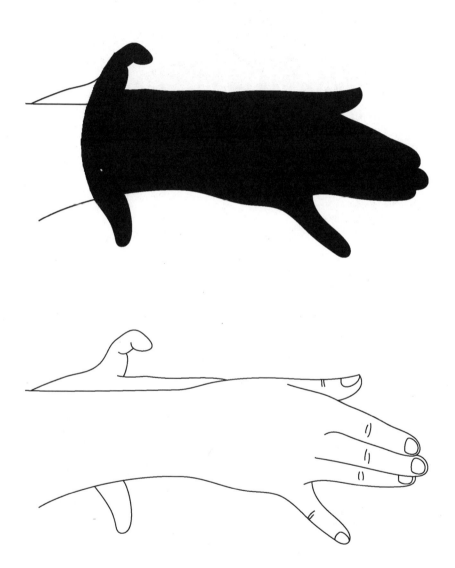

PONY

SUGGESTIONS: Moving your thumbs slightly will mimic the flicking motion of a pony's ears. Open and close the mouth by moving your little fingers up and down. Try to recreate the way a pony behaves by rolling the nose up towards the sky and letting out a loud neighing sound. You can also show the pony grazing in a field by rolling the nose downward and making chewing movements.

RABBIT

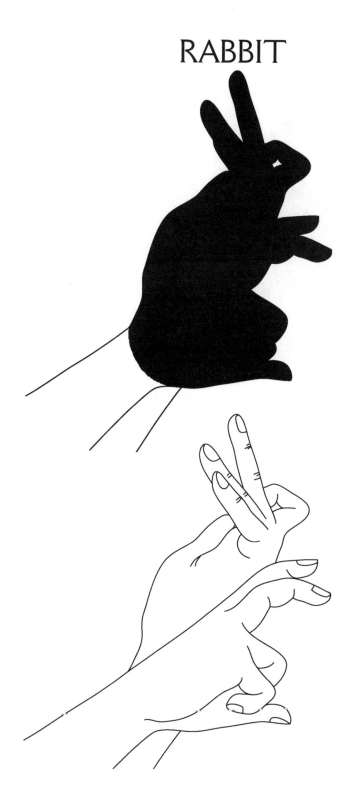

RABBIT HEAD

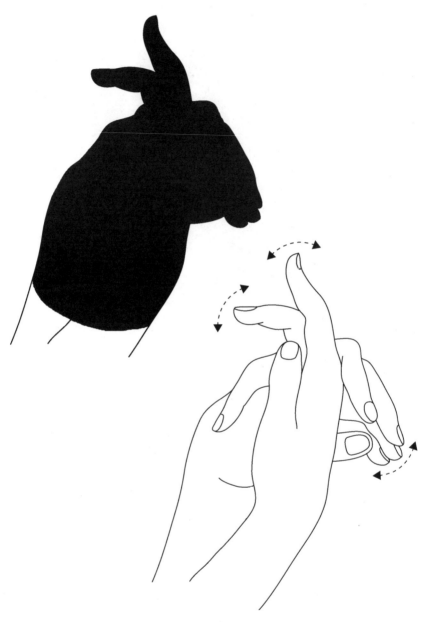

SUGGESTIONS: You can move the rabbit's ears by moving the index and middle fingers of your right hand. Make the rabbit's nose twitch by making very slight up and down movements with the bunched fingers of your left hand.

SNAIL

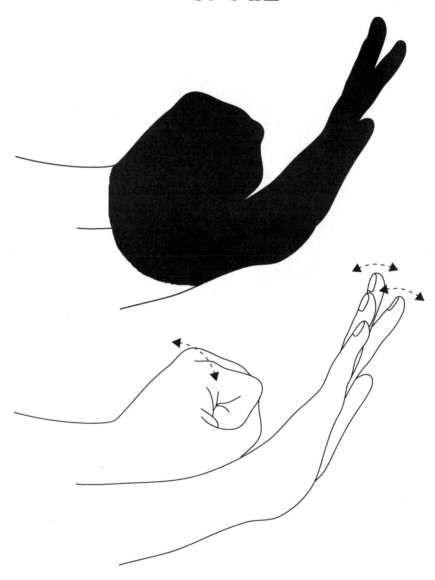

SUGGESTIONS: While holding your hands in position, move the snail VERY slowly across the screen to give it a forward motion. At the same time, rock the fist of your left hand from side-to-side to make the snail's shell appear to sway as it lumbers forward. Every once and a while stop and move the fingers of your right hand forward and back to mimic the movement of the snail's tentacles.

SNAKE

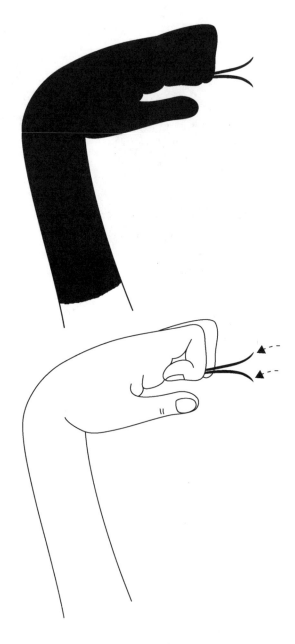

SUGGESTIONS: Cut two thin strips of paper and position them between your first and middle fingers. They will look like the snake's flickering tongue.

TURTLE

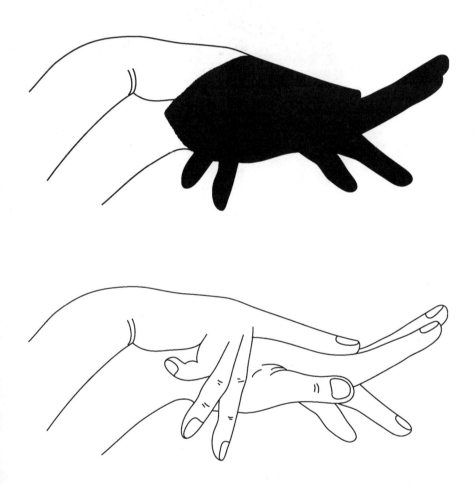

WOLF HOWLING

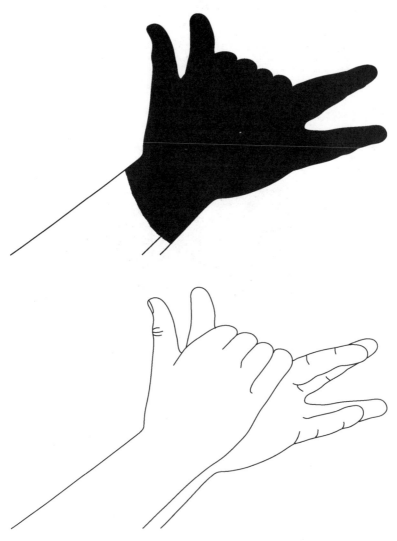

SUGGESTIONS: Add realism to this hand shadow by rolling the nose up towards the sky and letting out a loud whoop and howl. When the howl is finished, lower the nose and close the mouth. Allow a few seconds of silence and then do it again. For added effect, have an assistant (or two) hide at the back of the room and answer to your howls with howls of their own. Since this is one of the ways that wolves communicate in nature, the effect will be very realistic. Imagine the surprise it will give your audience when wolves start howling all around the room!

YOUNG BUCK

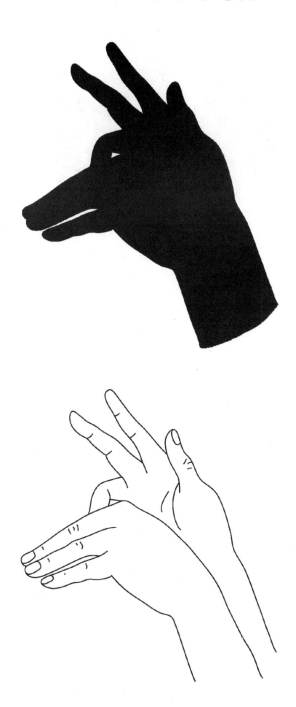

BIRD FLYING

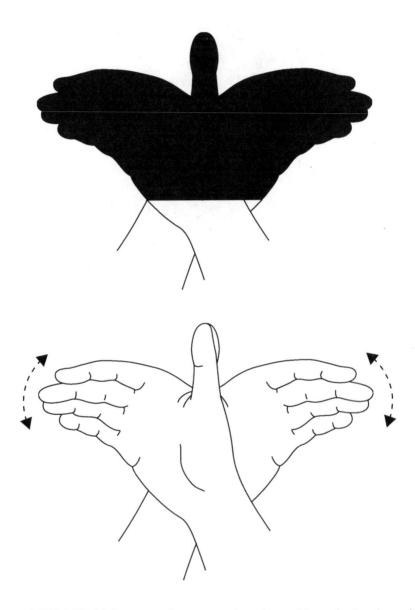

SUGGESTIONS: When you have your hands positioned, simply make a waving motion with both of your hands (keeping your thumbs overlapped as shown) to make the bird appear to be flying. At the same time, sway and dip back and forth across the screen.

COCKATOO

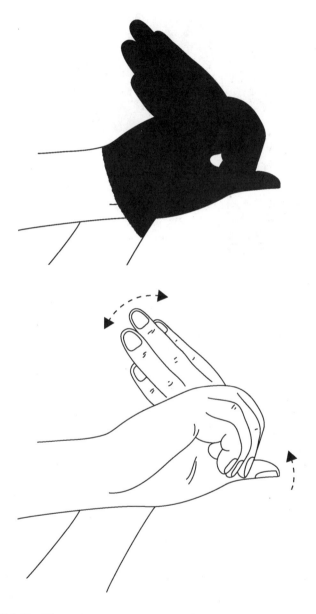

SUGGESTIONS: To make the cockatoo bow, hold your position and roll both hands forward. Wave the fingers of the left hand to make him flex his crest. To make it look like it is eating, simply bend the thumb of the right hand up and down.

GOOSE

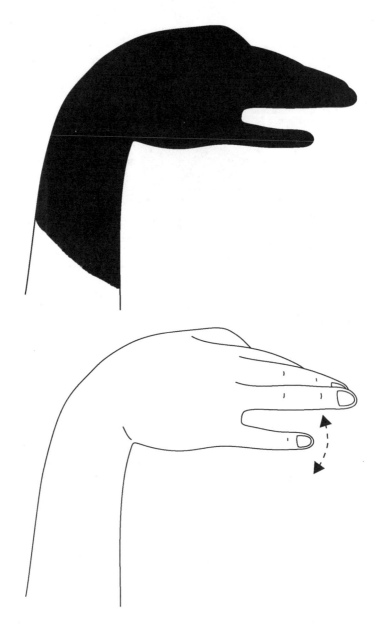

SUGGESTIONS: You can open and shut the goose's beak by moving your little finger up and down (it takes a bit of practice). While holding the position, dip your hand forward and down to make it look like the goose is pecking on the ground.

HEN

SUGGESTIONS: Bring this amusing hand shadow to life by swinging the thumbs away from each other and then back together again. Make a hen's "cluck, cluck, cluck" sound at the same time.

PARROT

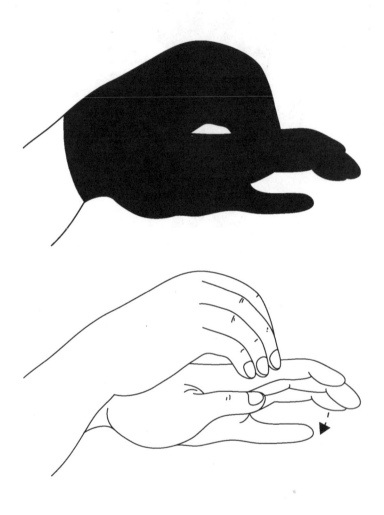

SUGGESTIONS: You can show how this parrot would eat a cracker by bringing the three fingers of the left hand down to the little finger. Mimic a parrot by saying "Polly wants a cracker" and have an assistant put a cracker in the beak.

ROOSTER

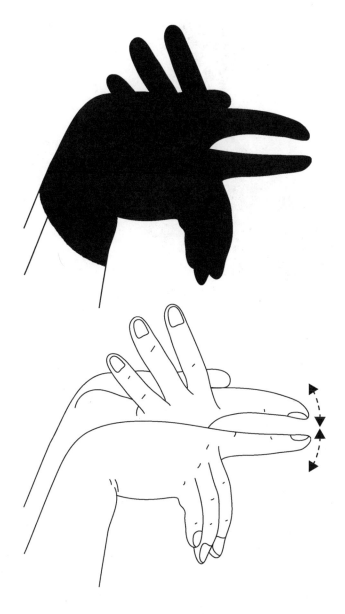

SUGGESTIONS: Most everyone knows the sound of a rooster crowing. If you make this sound while opening and shutting the first fingers of both hands (to make the beak open and close), this hand shadow will appear to be very life-like.

SWAN

SUGGESTIONS: While holding the position shown, gently rock forward and back to give the illusion of floating on water. Try dipping the head forward to make it look like it is drinking. If you are ambitious, swing the beak around and into the tail area and open and close the fingers of the left hand at the same time (see diagram in circle). It will give the appearance of a swan preening its tail feathers.

42

TURKEY

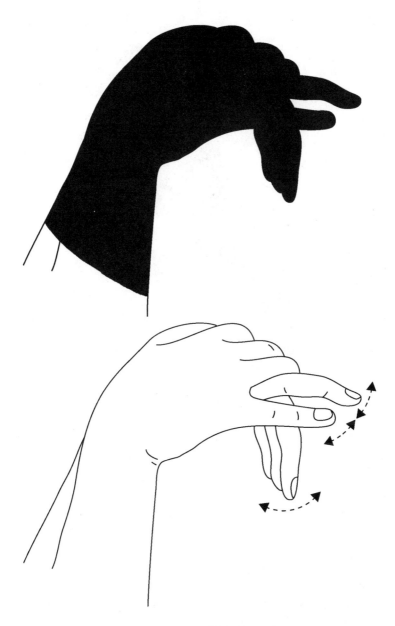

SUGGESTIONS: Make this turkey gobble by moving the first finger of your left hand up and down against the little finger of your right hand. At the same time, swing the three hanging fingers of your left hand to make the turkey's wattle shake.

WOODPECKER

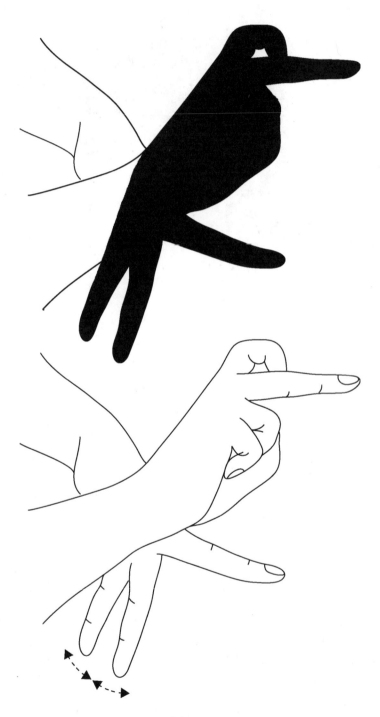

FACES

Here are a few basic instructions for making hand shadow faces. It takes both hands. One hand is used to form the profile of the face (chin, lips and nose) as shown in Fig. 1. The other hand forms the profile of the forehead and head (on some characters, hats or hair) as shown in Fig. 2.

Not all hand shadow faces are made exactly like the drawings below but once you learn these basics, you will be able to experiment with different positions and come up with your own hand shadow characters.

Fig. 1

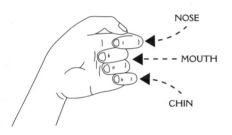

NOSE

MOUTH

CHIN

Use hand #1 to form
the features of the face.

Fig. 2

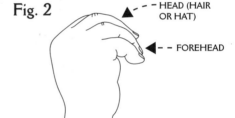

HEAD (HAIR OR HAT)

FOREHEAD

Use hand #2 to form
the head and forehead.

Fig. 3

Position the head on top of the face.
Leave a small opening for the eye.

Fig. 4

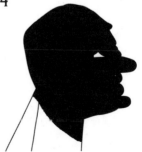

The basic hand shadow face
may look something like this.

A KING WITH HIS CROWN

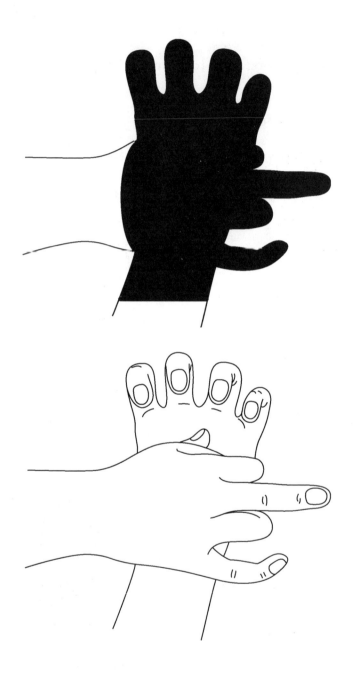

BASEBALL PLAYER

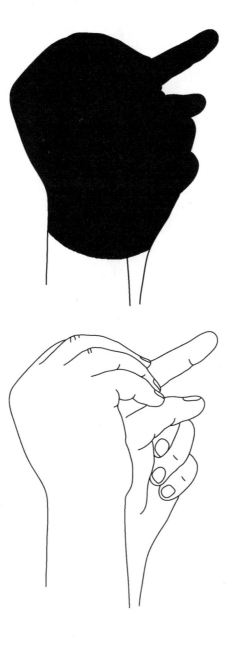

SUGGESTIONS: You can make this fellow look up, to follow the ball, and down, to watch the catch, by holding the position and rolling your hands forward and back at the wrists in the direction of the cap peak.

CLOWN

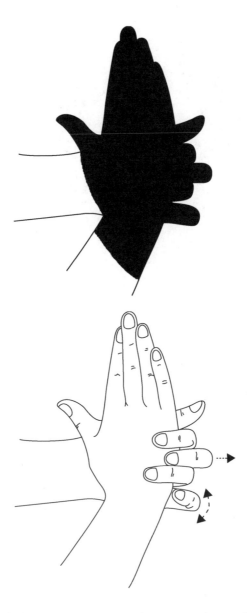

SUGGESTIONS: If you want to catch your audience by surprise, you can slowly open out the middle finger of your left hand. This will make it looks as if his nose is slowly growing bigger and bigger. If you can wiggle the little finger of the left hand up and down, you can make him appear to be laughing.

COWBOY

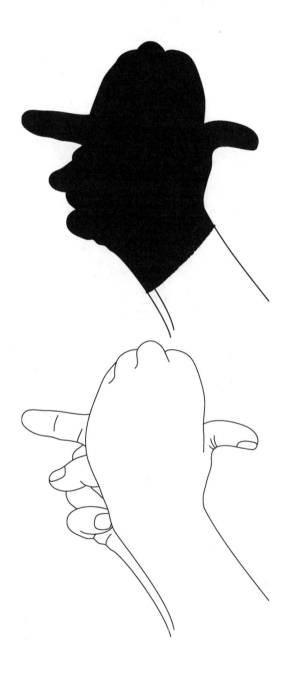

GRANDFATHER IN
HIS OLD HAT

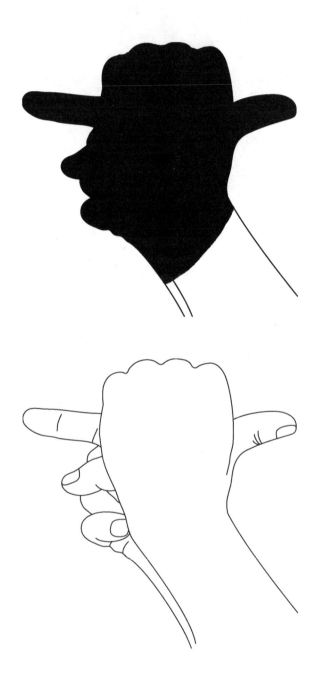

GRANDMOTHER IN
HER NEW HAT

JESTER

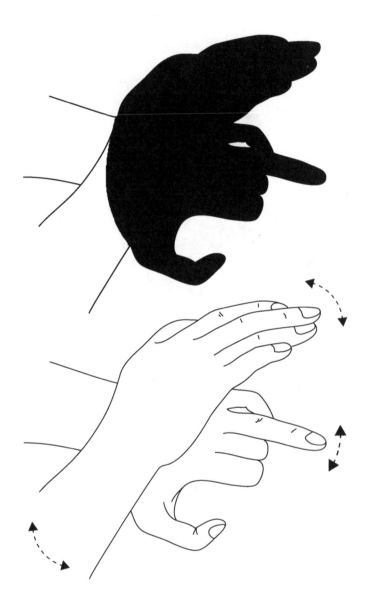

SUGGESTIONS: Make the jester's nose wiggle by wiggling the third finger on your left hand. Make his hat bob around by holding the position of your right hand and gently rocking it back and forth.

52

THE SEA CAPTAIN

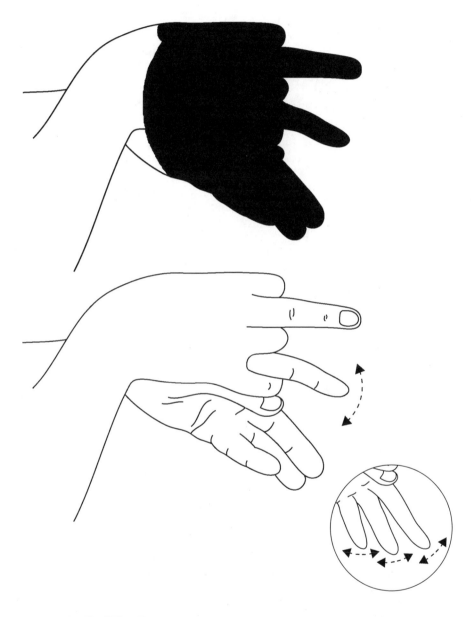

SUGGESTIONS: The first finger of the left hand forms the captain's nose. Wiggle it to wiggle the nose. If you open and close the middle, ring and little fingers of the left hand that form the beard (see diagram in circle), you will make his whiskers wag in the sea breeze.

Publications by Algrove Publishing Limited

The following is a list of titles from our popular *"Classic Reprint Series"* as well as other publications by Algrove Publishing Limited.

ARCHITECTURE, BUILDING, AND DESIGN

Item #		Title
49L8096	☐	A GLOSSARY OF TERMS USED IN ENGLISH ARCHITECTURE
49L8137	☐	AUDELS CARPENTERS AND BUILDERS GUIDE - *VOLS. 1-4*
49L8016	☐	BARN PLANS & OUTBUILDINGS
49L8046	☐	BEAUTIFYING THE HOME GROUNDS
49L8112	☐	BUILDING WITH LOGS AND LOG CABIN CONSTRUCTION
49L8092	☐	DETAIL, COTTAGE AND CONSTRUCTIVE ARCHITECTURE
49L8015	☐	FENCES, GATES & BRIDGES
49L8706	☐	FROM LOG TO LOG HOUSE
49L0720	☐	HOMES & INTERIORS OF THE 1920'S
49L8111	☐	LOW-COST WOOD HOMES
49L8030	☐	SHELTERS, SHACKS & SHANTIES
49L8139	☐	THE STAIR BUILDERS' GUIDE
49L8050	☐	STRONG'S BOOK OF DESIGNS
49L8064	☐	THE ARCHITECTURE OF COUNTRY HOUSES
49L8023	☐	THE OPEN TIMBER ROOFS OF THE MIDDLE AGES

CLASSIC CATALOGS

Item #		Title
49L8004	☐	BOULTON & PAUL, LTD. 1898 CATALOGUE
49L8098	☐	CATALOG OF MISSION FURNITURE 1913 – *COME-PACKT FURNITURE*
49L8097	☐	MASSEY-HARRIS CIRCA 1914 CATALOG
49L8089	☐	OVERSHOT WATER WHEELS FOR SMALL STREAMS
49L8079	☐	WILLIAM BULLOCK & CO. – *HARDWARE CATALOG, CIRCA 1850*

GARDENING

Item #		Title
49L8082	☐	CANADIAN WILD FLOWERS (C. P. TRAILL)
49L8113	☐	COLLECTING SEEDS OF WILD PLANTS AND SHIPPING LIVE PLANT MATERIAL
49L8029	☐	FARM WEEDS OF CANADA
49L8056	☐	FLORA'S LEXICON
49L8705	☐	REFLECTIONS ON THE FUNGALOIDS
49L8057	☐	THE WILDFLOWERS OF CANADA

HUMOR AND PUZZLES

Item #		Title
49L8074	☐	ARE YOU A GENIUS? WHAT IS YOUR I.Q?
49L8106	☐	CLASSIC COWBOY CARTOONS, VOL. 1 (J.R. WILLIAMS)
49L8109	☐	CLASSIC COWBOY CARTOONS, VOL. 2 (J.R. WILLIAMS)
49L8118	☐	CLASSIC COWBOY CARTOONS, VOL. 3 (J.R. WILLIAMS)
49L8119	☐	CLASSIC COWBOY CARTOONS, VOL. 4 (J.R. WILLIAMS)
49L8072	☐	CLASSIC PUZZLES AND HOW TO SOLVE THEM
49L8103	☐	GRANDMOTHER'S PUZZLE BOOK 1
49L8142	☐	GRANDMOTHER'S PUZZLE BOOK 2
49L8127	☐	JOIN THE DOTS PUZZLE BOOKS
49L8081	☐	MR. PUNCH WITH ROD AND GUN – *THE HUMOUR OF FISHING AND SHOOTING*
49L8073	☐	NAME IT! THE PICTORIAL QUIZ BOOK
49L8126	☐	OUR BOARDING HOUSE WITH MAJOR HOOPLE – *1927*
49L8125	☐	OUT OUR WAY–*SAMPLER 20s, 30s & 40s* (J.R. WILLIAMS)
49L8044	☐	SAM LOYD'S PICTURE PUZZLES
49L8084	☐	THE ART OF ARTHUR WATTS
49L8071	☐	THE BULL OF THE WOODS, VOL. 1 (J.R. WILLIAMS)
49L8080	☐	THE BULL OF THE WOODS, VOL. 2 (J.R. WILLIAMS)
49L8104	☐	THE BULL OF THE WOODS, VOL. 3 (J.R. WILLIAMS)
49L8114	☐	THE BULL OF THE WOODS, VOL. 4 (J.R. WILLIAMS)
49L8115	☐	THE BULL OF THE WOODS, VOL. 5 (J.R. WILLIAMS)
49L8116	☐	THE BULL OF THE WOODS, VOL. 6 (J.R. WILLIAMS)
49I8128	☐	THE NIGHT BEFORE CHRISTMAS WITH PUZZLE PICTURES
49L8107	☐	U.S. CAVALRY CARTOONS (J.R. WILLIAMS)

NAVAL AND MARINE

Item #		Title
49L8090	☐	BOAT-BUILDING AND BOATING
49L8707	☐	BUILDING THE NORWEGIAN SAILING PRAM *(MANUAL AND PLANS)*
49L8708	☐	BUILDING THE SEA URCHIN *(MANUAL AND PLANS)*
49L8138	☐	HOW SAILS ARE MADE AND HANDLED
49L8078	☐	MANUAL OF SEAMANSHIP FOR BOYS AND SEAMEN OF THE ROYAL NAVY, 1904
49L8129	☐	OLD SHIP FIGURE-HEADS & STERNS
49L8095	☐	SAILING SHIPS AT A GLANCE
49L8134	☐	SAILING VESSEL SILHOUETTES
49I8144	☐	THE KEDGE-ANCHOR
49L8099	☐	THE SAILOR'S WORD-BOOK
49L8605	☐	THE SAILOR'S POCKET BOOK OF KNOTS
49L8058	☐	THE YANKEE WHALER
49L8025	☐	THE YOUNG SEA OFFICER'S SHEET ANCHOR
49L8061	☐	TRADITIONS OF THE NAVY

REFERENCE

Item #		Title
49L8024	☐	1800 MECHANICAL MOVEMENTS AND DEVICES
49L8093	☐	507 MECHANICAL MOVEMENTS
49L8055	☐	970 MECHANICAL APPLIANCES AND NOVELTIES OF CONSTRUCTION
49L8602	☐	ALL THE KNOTS YOU NEED
49L8083	☐	AMERICAN MECHANICAL DICTIONARY – KNIGHT VOL. I, VOL. II, VOL. III
49L8077	☐	CAMP COOKERY
49L8711	☐	DESIGNING SUNDIALS – *THE GRAPHIC METHOD*
49L8145	☐	HAWKINS' MECHANICAL DICTIONARY
49L8001	☐	LEE'S PRICELESS RECIPES
49L8135	☐	MUSSON'S IMPROVED LUMBER AND LOG POCKET BOOK
49L8018	☐	THE BOY'S BOOK OF MECHANICAL MODELS
49L8610	☐	THE CLASSIC ART OF HAND SHADOWS
49L8019	☐	WINDMILLS AND WIND MOTORS

TRADES

Item #		Title
49L8014	☐	BOOK OF TRADES
49L8086	☐	FARM BLACKSMITHING
49L8031	☐	FARM MECHANICS
49L8141	☐	FARM WORKSHOP GUIDE
49L8087	☐	FORGING
49L8027	☐	HANDY FARM DEVICES AND HOW TO MAKE THEM
49L8002	☐	HOW TO PAINT SIGNS & SHO' CARDS
49L8054	☐	HOW TO USE THE STEEL SQUARE
49L8094	☐	THE YOUNG MILL-WRIGHT AND MILLER'S GUIDE

WOODWORKING AND CRAFTS

Item #		Title
49L8130	☐	50 POPULAR WOODWORKING PROJECTS
49L8012	☐	BOY CRAFT
49L8110	☐	CHAIN SAW AND CROSSCUT SAW TRAINING COURSE
49L8048	☐	CLAY MODELLING AND PLASTER CASTING
49L8005	☐	COLONIAL FURNITURE
49L8065	☐	COPING SAW WORK
49L8032	☐	DECORATIVE CARVING, PYROGRAPHY AND FLEMISH CARVING
49L8091	☐	FURNITURE DESIGNING AND DRAUGHTING
49L8049	☐	HANDBOOK OF TURNING
49L8020	☐	MISSION FURNITURE, HOW TO MAKE IT
49L8710	☐	QUEEN ANNE FURNITURE - *HISTORY, DESIGN & CONSTRUCTION*
49L8033	☐	ORNAMENTAL AND DECORATIVE WOOD CARVINGS
49L8003	☐	RUSTIC CARPENTRY
49L8085	☐	SKELETON LEAVES AND PHANTOM FLOWERS
49L8068	☐	SPECIALIZED JOINERY
49L8052	☐	STANLEY COMBINATION PLANES –*THE 45, THE 50 & THE 55*
49L8034	☐	THE ART OF WHITTLING
49L8131	☐	TIN-CAN PROJECTS AND ART-METAL WORK
49L8042	☐	TURNING FOR AMATEURS
49L8067	☐	WOOD HANDBOOK – *WOOD AS AN ENGINEERING MATERIAL*
49L8060	☐	WOODEN PLANES AND HOW TO MAKE THEM
49L8013	☐	YOU CAN MAKE IT
49L8035	☐	YOU CAN MAKE IT FOR CAMP & COTTAGE
49L8036	☐	YOU CAN MAKE IT FOR PROFIT

Algrove Publishing Limited, 36 Mill Street, P.O. Box 1238, Almonte, Ontario, Canada K0A 1A0
Telephone: (613) 256-0350 Fax: (613) 256-0360 Email: sales@algrove.com Web: www.algrove.com